DEAR PARENTS PLEASE...

*Your kids want to talk
with you about
alcohol and other drugs*

DEAR PARENTS PLEASE...

*Your kids want to talk
with you about
alcohol and other drugs*

By Donald Cutler

BROADHEARTH
PUBLISHING
1995

DEAR PARENTS PLEASE ...*Your kids want to talk with you about alcohol and other drugs*

Copyright ©1995 by Donald Cutler
Manufactured in the United States of America
First Edition

All rights reserved. No part of this book may be reproduced in any form or by any means without express permission in writing from the author

>Donald Cutler
>26 Cross Street
>Needham, MA 02194
>Tel. 617/444-6969

with the exception of brief quotations in critical articles and reviews. However, critical correspondence and discussion will be welcomed by the author at the above address.

> The information contained in *Dear Parents Please...Your kids want to talk with you about alcohol and other drugs* is meant to provide the reader with information about drug misuse and its prevention. While the information contained herein is believed to be correct, this is not a medical text. Broadhearth Publishing accepts no responsibility for any errors or omissions nor can it be responsible for any damages arising from the use of this book.

Graphic Design & Typography by Jeff Farr

Library of Congress Catalog Card Number:
95-077904

International Standard Book No. 0-9647081-1-6

Published by
Broadhearth Publishing
26 Cross Street
Needham, MA 02194
Tel. 617/444-6969

This book is dedicated with admiration
and affection to the men and women,
past and present, of the FCD Educational
Services, Inc., teaching staff. While sharing
their own special knowledge of addiction,
and working with compassion and
commitment, they have provided alcohol,
nicotine, and other drug education for
hundreds of thousands of people of
all ages.

DEDICATION

ACKNOWLEDGEMENTS

Much of what is in *Dear Parents Please...* has come from the experiences and ideas developed at the nonprofit FCD Educational Services, Inc. (Freedom from Chemical Dependency) since its formation in 1976. The list of other foundations, corporations, and individuals who support FCD financially would cover several pages. This help continues to be all important. There could not be a more loyal group than the FCD Trustees, several of whom have served since the earliest days. Their wisdom and advice is vitally important. Encouragement and help have come also from many other individuals. Without the urging and encouragement of Mrs. Jessie Sargent, FCD would never have gotten away from the starting line. Eliot Dalton, a close friend since our schoolboy days joined up as fund-raiser and partner. Bill Chamberlin, an FCD Trustee since 1977 and now the Assistant Headmaster of Noble and Greenough School in Dedham, Massachusetts had the idea for the format and much of the content of the original FCD four-day Alcohol Education Course. Joseph Ippolito, past Trustee and District Superintendent in the Boston Public School system helped FCD become an important resource to inner city schools. Kelley Sassano of the Weymouth Center in Southern Pines, N.C., was able to decipher, and type the original long hand manuscript. Most importantly, without the love and understanding of my wife, Lloyd, and all the other members of my family, neither FCD nor this book would have happened. My thanks and gratitude to you all.

ABOUT THE AUTHOR AND FCD

My credentials for writing about prevention education are earned both from personal experience with alcohol addiction, and from nearly twenty years of working with children in public and private schools throughout the United States and in many countries abroad.

Alcohol had caused great trouble for me and my last drink was swallowed in 1975. Soon thereafter, I set out to learn about the disease of alcoholism and, after a year of study, founded the non-profit organization Freedom from Chemical Dependency Educational Services, Inc. (FCD).

FCD began as a place where families, troubled by an alcoholic in their midst, could learn the facts and be guided in carrying out a family intervention program aimed at getting their alcoholic to accept help.

Our work with families led to an invitation to teach students in a local independent school and it did not take us long to become alcohol and drug education consultants to a number of schools in the Boston area.

This is how I found myself being a classroom teacher at the age of 62 — a far cry from the electronics industry where I had spent 35 years in management. I have felt an enormous sense of gratitude and wonderment as FCD has become better and better known. Its *Comprehensive Four Day Course* is standard prevention fare at hundreds of public and independent schools throughout the United States, Europe and Asia. Our teaching staff has met with hundreds of thousands of students, many of their teachers, and a sprinkling of their parents.

ABOUT THE AUTHOR AND FCD

Credit for FCD becoming the world's foremost organization of its kind must go to the men and women of our teaching staff. All of them have recovered from alcoholism, and/or some other drug dependency and have achieved years of solid sobriety. They are highly trained and very professional in their work. They teach with great compassion and caring, with the goal of preventing others from suffering as they did. Written critiques of their work by students are *97% positive* — an astounding figure. A common theme appears over and over, *"Thanks, I learned a lot, and it was good to hear it from someone who has been there."*

WHY THIS BOOK WAS WRITTEN

While alcohol and drug prevention workshops for school faculty and other segments of the school community have been well received, **scheduled meetings for parents often turn out to be *disastrous* as far as attendance is concerned.**

A school can make elaborate plans with lots of publicity for a parent meeting only to have a handful of them show up. And these are often the ones who are already knowledgeable and do not need to be there. **Lack of parent interest continues to be the major frustration of FCD.**

This must stop. **Parents *must* take responsibility for prevention education.** This book was written to give parents the tools to do just that.

I am amazed at my venturesomeness in attempting even a small book project. But I feel there has to be a basic change in how to cut the demand for alcohol and other drugs. This book is based on 20 years of FCD's and my own experiences working with children.

And one thing is clear. Your children want to talk with you about alcohol and drugs. They are looking to you for guidance.

HOW TO USE THIS BOOK

I have tried to keep this book as short as possible. Its purpose is simple — to give you the information you need to keep an open dialogue with your children regarding the use of alcohol and drugs. And if you think this subject may be too difficult, it's not. You will find the reading easy and descriptions nontechnical. You don't need to be a doctor or pharmacologist to understand this subject and you don't need to be a psychologist to be successful in preventing drug misuse in your family. You just need the desire to learn and to do your part.

I strongly suggest that you read the entire book through once. It will give you a solid background on the problems associated with alcohol and drug misuse. The first few chapters are particularly important. They describe how a young person can become chemically dependent and why a family policy of non use — and early intervention when use *does* occur — is the best defense. Since alcohol is the most widely misused drug, I have used it as a "template" in discussing the general aspects of drug misuse and addiction. But keep in mind, you can plug in *any* drug and the major principles will still apply. Specific information on other commonly misused drugs can be found in later chapters.

I like to think of this book as "interactive." It is made to be *used*. Be sure to keep a highlighter pen handy so you can highlight points that particularly apply to you. Everyone's situation is different. Use the comment sections — found on nearly every page — to record your own thoughts and to "customize" this book to you and your family.

Prevention education is an ongoing process and we are *all* still learning. DEAR PARENTS PLEASE...is your reference and guide. Refer to it when needed — and if you need additional information, or hands-on help — check the resources listed in the back of this book. Remember, you are not alone in this fight!

HOW TO USE THIS BOOK

CONTENTS

About The Author and FCD	8
Why This Book Was Written	11
How To Use This Book	12
Introduction	17
Alcohol and Other Mood Altering Drugs in American Schools	19
Some General Information You'll Need	23
Talking With Your Child About Alcohol and Other Drugs Is Easier Than You Think	24
The First Step: Learning The Facts	25
How Do You Know If Someone Is In Trouble?	29
Facing the Challenge	30
Talking About Alcohol and Other Drugs With Your Child	33
The Long Haul	39
Alcohol: From Social Drinking To Addiction	43
Nicotine	57
Marijuana	63
Other Drugs	
STIMULANTS	
Cocaine and Crack	76
Amphetamines	80
HALLUCINOGENS	
LSD	82
PCP / Phencyclidine	85
Mescaline / Peyote	87
MDMA	88
Psilocybin	89
NARCOTICS	
Opiates	90
Heroin	91

SEDATIVES AND HYPNOTICS
Barbiturates 93
Benzodiazepines 93
Methaqualone 94
INHALANTS
Glues, Solvents and Aerosols 96
Nitrous Oxide 96
Nitrites 97
STEROIDS
Anabolic Steroids 99
Family Intervention 103
Final thoughts On
Connected Issues 109
Supporting The Non-User 110
Teaching Children Responsible
Drinking — A Bad Idea 111
Moderate Drinking
— A Grown-Ups Right 112
A Wiser "War on Drugs" 113
Postscript 114
Suggested Reading 117
Additional Resources 121

CONTENTS

DEAR PARENTS PLEASE...

Introduction

...Your kids want to talk with you about alcohol and other drugs

Everyone knows that alcohol and other drugs are playing havoc with one generation of children after another. This is a health problem of epidemic size with no good solution in sight.

With all the media attention, you would think parents would have become the *leading force* in teaching their children why the use of alcohol or other drugs can be so ruinous to a young person's health.

Not so. Most parents are content to sit on the sidelines — wringing their hands from time to time — but becoming involved only if trouble strikes at home. Education having to do with alcohol and other drugs is left to the schools which are already overburdened without this added responsibility.

What properly should have been a family obligation, has been defaulted for some unsound reasons. Two of the main ones are:

1. *It is very difficult for parents to talk to their kids about alcohol and other drugs.*
Not true. Children want to talk as long as it's *real* talk....not "Just say no" or "Don't use them. They are bad for you and you are bad if you do."

2. *It's difficult and time consuming to learn the facts which make alcohol and other drugs so dangerous.*
Not true. A few hours of effort will give parents the knowledge they need to talk with their children sensibly about the reasons for being non-users during all the growing-up years.

When such talks are tied to love for the child and concern for his or her health, there is a good chance that a family prohibition rule will work throughout the adolescent years.

Notes, Comments & Ideas

Alcohol and Other Mood Altering Drugs in American Schools

We recently heard from friends living abroad. They have two children, a 10-year-old girl and a boy, 12. They had read upsetting accounts of the drug scene in American schools. Since the father's job is changing, and they will be returning to the States, they wanted to know what I thought. Here is what I wrote:

Dear Phil and Peggy:

I wish it were possible to answer your letter by saying that alcohol and other drug use by school children is on the way out. I'm sorry to say such is not the case. It would be difficult to find a school here that has not been touched by the problem. Inner city communities get the most media attention because of drug related violence, but don't think that suburban towns, and supposedly bucolic country villages are free of trouble. It's like a plague that's swept the country — it's everywhere. Do all kids use? Certainly not; I'm skeptical of published percentages and numbers, but it seems about one-half of all school-aged kids have chosen not to use at all. The other half drink and use drugs in varying degrees — from the occasional party user, to the chronic or habitual user, to a small percent who have become addicted and whose lives are in jeopardy.

You should know that your 10 and 12-year-olds are probably going to get into situations where alcohol, nicotine, marijuana and perhaps other drugs are being used. It doesn't seem possible that drug use would touch the lives of children below the fifth grade, but unfortunately, nowadays it does. The age level of drug and alcohol users has been going down year after year, and we are now doing prevention education with more and more children in grades K–5; it appears it's never too soon to start! You asked what position we've taken in

Notes, Comments & Ideas

*the face of all this. As you know, we are not prohibitionists, we see nothing wrong with legal drinking in moderation. We do not condone breaking laws which affect children under 21, and for **health reasons, we teach abstinence from all drugs, particularly alcohol and nicotine, during all the growing-up years.** This is often a far out thought I'm sorry to say.*

Government estimates indicate several million adolescents are in trouble with alcohol and a tragic feature of teenage drinking is weekend parties where drinking to get drunk is accepted and expected.

Marijuana use is down a bit but is still common. Negative scientific findings on how it affects the reproduction and immune systems have scared off some users.

I expect you've read about our government's War on Drugs, which is aimed at shutting off drug supplies from abroad — particularly cocaine. While there have been successes, the effort has been disappointing. Someone recently wrote that shutting down the Andean drug trade was like trying to put the Japanese out of the automobile business. Interestingly, the War on Drugs does not target alcohol, which causes many times more teenage problems than cocaine or crack cocaine. It appears what is needed is a much greater emphasis on reducing the demand through prevention education.

When we started in 1976, many heads of schools had trouble admitting their students were using anything stronger than soda-pop. They resisted adding alcohol and drug education courses for fear of looking bad or to avoid criticism from parents who might not want their children exposed to the subject. Things have changed dramatically and now it is rare

Notes, Comments & Ideas

to find a school without some kind of prevention education program. Effectiveness varies greatly depending on the commitment of the head of the school.

You see, schools have been forced into the alcohol and drug education business because parents have nearly always defaulted on a responsibility that clearly should have been theirs. I think there are several reasons why this happened, not the least of which was the fact that "don't" was all that parents had to offer their children as advice on the subject. This is not too surprising as we are dealing with a relatively new phenomenon spawned to a great extent during the 60's. And until recently, one did not talk openly about alcoholism or drug addiction. These subjects were considered shameful, disgraceful, and signs of moral weakness. Nowadays, chemical dependency is a common term and alcohol and drug addiction is more easily discussed. This is a major step forward, and now it is time for parents to take responsibility for the solution to a devastating health problem. To do so, they have to learn the facts, so they can say much more than "don't." Fortunately, this is not difficult or time consuming; one half day of study should convince any parent that no effort is too great when its objective is to keep their children alcohol and drug free during their school years.

I look forward to hearing from you on your return and will be glad to make some suggestions which you may find helpful as you start talking with your children about alcohol and other drugs.

Sincerely,

Don

Notes, Comments & Ideas

Some General Information You'll Need

TALKING TO YOUR CHILDREN ABOUT ALCOHOL AND DRUGS IS EASIER THAN YOU THINK

Notes, Comments & Ideas

Walter Cronkite — on the radio to kick off the national non-profit "Partnership for a Drug Free America" — pleads with parents to talk to their children about drugs. No matter, he says, how difficult it may be, even if it is harder than discussing sex!

The truth is Mr. Cronkite is partially wrong. Talking to your children about alcohol and drugs may not be difficult at all — young people *want* to talk to their parents about alcohol and other drugs.

In commenting about our work, thousands of high school students have written, "I wouldn't mind talking to my parents about this, but all they say is `Don't'."

Middle school children are even more open and willing to talk. Mrs. Reagan's *"Just say no"* is a favorite expression of small children, who, incidentally, have an amazing amount of information (much of it inaccurate) they would like to share with grown-ups. Unfortunately, the older the child, the more inadequate "Just say no" becomes, and kids of middle and high school age just think it a joke.

Recently, at a middle school in a central Massachusetts community, a senior FCD teacher presented an evening of education for a good-sized group of both parents and their children. After the ice was broken, our teacher had very little to do as the meeting developed into an exchange of views and beliefs between the students and parents. Issues important to each were discussed, mostly in an objective way.

DEAR PARENTS PLEASE...

SOME GENERAL INFORMATION YOU'LL NEED

This was a first for nearly everyone involved. Astonishingly, the most common student comment was a loud and clear, **"Parents, we want you to talk with us about drinking or doing drugs. We need to talk together. But please say more than `don't'."**

The disease of alcoholism and other drug addiction has come out from under the rug and can be more easily discussed. Treatment facilities mushroomed during the 70's and 80's, as did the number of books written on the subject. Every aspect has been covered many times over. Our goal is to keep material as brief and simple as possible but with enough detail to empower you to successfully prohibit alcohol and drug use by your children.

THE FIRST STEP: LEARNING THE FACTS

Since the use of alcohol by American children exceeds the combined total use of all other mood altering drugs many times over, we shall use alcohol as the centerpiece in giving you various facts, definitions and descriptions. However, you should also remember that much of what we have to say about alcohol misuse and addiction applies to other drugs as well.

An up-to-date definition of alcoholism was published in the *Journal of the American Medical Association* in 1992. It reflects research conducted since 1976 and comes from leading experts in the field:

Alcoholism is a primary, chronic disease with genetic, psychosocial, and environmental factors influencing its development and manifestations. The disease is often progressive

Notes, Comments & Ideas

and fatal. It is characterized by impaired control over drinking, preoccupation with the drug alcohol, use of alcohol despite adverse consequences, and distortions in thinking, most notably, denial. Each of these symptoms may be continuous or periodic.

Some clarification of this definition seems in order:

Primary Disease — A disease all by itself. It is not a symptom of some other disease.

Chronic — Once you get it you have got it for all time. We believe you can get well through total abstinence, but you are never cured and must never try drinking again!

Genetic — Without question, the disease runs in families and crops up in some family member or members of succeeding generations. The popular belief is that a child of an alcoholic parent or parents has a four times better chance of getting the disease than a child whose parents are moderate social drinkers or do not drink at all.

Psychosocial — Someone who maybe psychologically constituted to be at risk has an even better chance of getting into trouble if liquor or other drugs are an important part of his or her social life.

Environmental — In some households, liquor is important and is part of almost every activity. In others, it is not used at all. The average is some place in between, weighted toward non-use. The child brought up in the home where alcohol is ever present is more susceptible to trouble during adolescence than one where there is moderate or no use.

Notes, Comments & Ideas

SOME GENERAL INFORMATION YOU'LL NEED

Progressive — There is a thin line between the heavy social drinker and the alcoholic. Once crossed, there is no return to normal drinking, and the addicted person can always count on things getting worse as the disease progresses.

Fatal — Alcoholism is a one hundred percent fatal disease in the sense that unless halted, death comes sooner and often in more traumatic ways than normally expected.

Had I written the 1992 definition, I would have included the fact that alcoholism is:

Treatable — those who suffer from it can recover, and though they will never be cured, they can live a full, normal, and productive life as long as they never drink again.

Not so long ago, public drunkenness was treated as a crime, and alcoholics were popularly perceived as rag-tag individuals living on big city streets — unshaven panhandlers in filthy clothes, begging money for "food," which in reality would consist of their next bottle of cheap wine. I well remember the looks of disbelief when I told my classes back in the 70's that these unfortunate sick souls represented less than four percent of the alcoholics in the U.S. According to government figures published recently, there are more than 12,000,000 people troubled by alcohol. On average, each alcoholic or chemically dependent person adversely affects the lives of at least three other "healthy" people because of his or her devious, sick and bizarre behavior.

Notes, Comments & Ideas

...Your kids want to talk with you about alcohol and other drugs

Notes, Comments & Ideas

I am sure any of you who have lived with an addicted person are saying "Amen" to this. These sick people make up a cross section of our population — the banker, the butcher, the baker, the mother, the doctor, the writer, the honor student, the athlete, the mentally impaired, the judge, the lawyer, and perhaps most alarmingly, thousands upon thousands of children. All are very ill and nearly all have ceased to grow emotionally, intellectually, or spiritually.

For the teenager, this means missing out on much of the incredibly important adolescent years when so much must be learned in order to fit and compete in the adult world. For example, meet Jim: Jim became addicted at 15 and was an active alcoholic until age 20, when he went for help. He has now been 100% alcohol-free for seven years. However, besides missing out on college, he is now only able to get low paying employment. You see, when Jim became an adult, he had to deal with the challenges of the grown-up world with the smarts of a 15-year-old boy. He has had to play catch-up and is still going through adolescence while in his twenties. This is painfully hard work. I have known too many people in Jim's shoes — wonderful looking adults on the outside and unsure kids on the inside, many with zero self-confidence.

In my day, drinking and doing drugs was just not part of the lives of school children. I often think how lucky I was to have grown up in those times. At least I had become a young adult in college before doing any drinking.

SOME GENERAL INFORMATION YOU'LL NEED

Formerly it was thought that the drinking career of an average alcoholic lasted around 15 years from start to finish. Today, we know how far off the mark this can be. Many teenaged alcoholics compress an entire drinking career into two years from start to finish and do not miss out on a single horror.

HOW DO YOU KNOW IF SOMEONE IS IN TROUBLE?

There are definitions galore. The one that I like has to do with trouble: If drinking interferes or causes trouble with a person's job, his or her relationship with family or friends, the law, or if alcohol causes physical or mental health problems and the person cannot see them and denies what is happening and keeps on drinking, then it is safe to assume that at best, he or she is harmfully dependent and could well be addicted.

How about the person who says, "I won't get into trouble, because I don't drink anything but beer — no hard stuff." This, unfortunately, is not true; it is the alcohol content which counts. A one and one-half ounce shot of 86 proof whiskey equals a five ounce glass of wine or a 12 ounce bottle of beer.

Alcohol is classified as a depressant; however, small amounts can act like a stimulant, making social situations more fun by adding self-confidence and lowering inhibitions. Drinking large amounts can cause alcohol to become a sedative, acting as an anesthetic like ether. Large amounts can cause a person to "pass out" and become unconscious. Drinking a large

Notes, Comments & Ideas

...Your kids want to talk with you about alcohol and other drugs

amount quickly, commonly known as "chug-a-lugging," "shotgunning" or "funneling" may result in a toxic coma and, at worst, death.

For most people, stopping at the end of a period of excessive drinking brings on withdrawal symptoms, including varying amounts of short term physical and mental pain, general feelings of depression, and uneasiness. These symptoms can become chronic and, depending on the amount and frequency of heavy drinking, causes alcohol to become a depressant. Had I known that alcohol ends up being a depressant, I hope I would have had the sense not to use it to relieve the stress and strain of business and other problems. All it did was make matters worse. The trouble was, nobody told me.

FACING THE CHALLENGE

Alcoholism is not a simple disease. It invades every part of a person and can cause physical, emotional and spiritual distress. How this happens is described in detail later on, but from my experience, if harmony does not exist between a person's physical, mental and spiritual being, then it is difficult to grow as a person. This is particularly true for someone going through adolescence. **Adding heavy use of alcohol or other drugs to a period of continuing change and confusion makes the road to adulthood far more difficult or often impossible.**

Notes, Comments & Ideas

SOME GENERAL INFORMATION YOU'LL NEED

Here are a few more facts you should know:

- Children in fourth grade are quite often pressured to drink or use some other types of drugs.
- It is estimated that 40% of all middle and high school students use occasionally.
- One out of three high school seniors drink heavily.
- Drinking and driving is the leading cause of death among 15-to-24 year olds.
- Drinking and drugging are the leading causes of suicide among adolescents.
- The majority of children learn their drinking habits from parents.
- Alcohol, marijuana and other drugs are easy for a teenager to get and are in plentiful supply.

A child who is a heavy user does not have to get addicted to become an intellectually and emotionally crippled adult. If this happens, the love, care, and money spent on the child's up-bringing will have been squandered. The victims are both you as parents and your child, **who may never reach his or her potential as an adult.**

So again, I believe **every young person has a right to know the facts** and **these facts are best taught by parents**. I further believe this can then be coupled with a successful family prohibition against drinking or using other drugs all through the school years.

Notes, Comments & Ideas

...Your kids want to talk with you about alcohol and other drugs

DEAR PARENTS PLEASE...

Talking About Alcohol and Other Drugs With Your Child

OPENING A DIALOGUE

Notes, Comments & Ideas

While I believe implicitly that children want to talk to you about alcohol and other drugs, I don't want to suggest detailed *rules* on how you can have successful discussions with your child. The purpose of this chapter is to give you a starting point. What follows are some ideas FCD teachers have found useful in their classroom work.

To begin with, **the younger the child, the easier it is to get things started.** Nearly 40% of FCD's work is now in elementary schools, and it is not unusual to teach children in kindergarten or first grade. I suspect that many parents will be amazed at how much seven or eight-year-olds know. A great deal of their information is inaccurate. We have found that asking questions and discussing the answers is a good way to get things going and also to correct misconceptions. Here are some good questions to ask:

What do you think of when I say drink?

What do you think of when I say adult drinking?

What is this stuff called alcohol?

Who drinks it?

Do all adults drink it?

Why do they drink it? When do they drink it?

Do teenagers drink it?

Do all teenagers drink?

Why?

How?

When?

Why shouldn't teenagers drink?

Is alcohol a drug?

What is a drug?

Who gives them to you?

What are bad drugs?

Who gives them to you?

What are some things that adults do that kids aren't allowed to do?

Why not?

Whether talking with a seven-year-old or with a youngster in mid-adolescence, the same basic rules apply:

- know the facts
- use them with love and concern for health

We believe non-use family rules will work if they are established for these reasons.

Here is an imaginary talk between seven-year-old Suzy and her mother:

"Suzy, you remember that daddy and I said we were going to find out more about the drugs kids are using? Well, we've spent a good bit of time learning about each one and what we were told is so scary that we want you to get to know all about them too. We'll talk about each one as we go along. But today, we are going to talk a little about what we should do as a family to make sure that alcohol and other drugs don't make you sick or hurt you in any way. You can't possibly know how much daddy

and I love you. We think you are a wonderful little girl and we are going to make sure you are as good as you can be at whatever you choose to do when you grow up. You are doing well in school, and your teachers are happy with you. Your father and I will always be here for you, and you can always count on our love and help. One of our most important jobs is to protect your health so you will grow up strong in both your body and your mind. We learned that right this minute there are millions of children who will not grow up and be as strong and bright as they should be because of the alcohol they drank or the other drugs they used. We aren't going to let this happen to you, and I'm sure you can understand why. It is because we love you and care so much about keeping you well. So, we've made a family rule which is: **You will never, ever, no matter what, do any drinking or taking drugs until you are grown up.** Then, we hope that you will drink very little and will only use drugs your doctor has given you. So remember, this rule: **NO ALCOHOL AND NO DRUGS!**"

Because they started when Suzy was only seven, her parents have good reason to believe their family prohibition rule will work. Obviously it must be reinforced with continuing talks — some of them about specific drugs. Suzy must also be supported as she reaches an age when the whole issue becomes complicated by some of her friends who think it would be fun to have Suzy join them in drinking and drugging.

Notes, Comments & Ideas

The prohibition rule becomes more difficult to enforce if it is put in place after a child has left the family nest and has been subjected to outside influences and peer pressure. But regardless of a child's age, successful conversations can be had if you:

- Know your facts
- Talk with, not at
- Don't lecture
- Be a good listener
- Keep the conversation focused on health issues and love for the child

You will be surprised at how well things can go if you know what you are talking about. You may even get thanked.

Notes, Comments & Ideas

...Your kids want to talk with you about alcohol and other drugs

DEAR PARENTS PLEASE...

The Long Haul

PREVENTION EDUCATION IS A CONTINUOUS PROCESS

How nice it would be if it were possible to have a talk or two with a young child and feel confident that the drinking and drugging problem had been solved with his or her promise not to use "ever, ever until I've grown up and then I'll only drink a little."

The trouble is parents are working against a stacked deck. The pressures for a child to drink or use other drugs are ever present and come from many sources. Parents must keep the education process going as a counter balance.

Without parental help, the average child may only receive a small amount of prevention education from over-worked school teachers or counselors. Occasionally they are assisted by specially trained policemen.

What these fine people can accomplish is limited by available time and the large number of children involved. Very little individual attention can be given a child unless he or she has become chemically dependent, is in trouble, and needs special help.

Students do hear that alcohol and drug use hurts their health, but these messages are not coupled with family concern and love, which would make them so much more powerful. Instead, kids are made to feel they are bad people if they drink or do drugs. This is counterproductive because it contradicts so much of what they see around them. Let's take a look at some of the things that influence children to do what they do:

Notes, Comments & Ideas

THE LONG HAUL

Notes, Comments & Ideas

1. They want to act grown up and do what grown ups do.

2. Drinking, smoking, and using other drugs are fun, and knowing that the law is being broken only makes it even more exciting. Anyway, many grown-ups are smoking pot and doing cocaine.

3. Older brothers and sisters drink and do drugs, and so do many friends. Some of these put pressure on younger kids to use.

4. Media/advertising glorifies drinking, often making drinkers appear to be great lovers and/or he-men. It also makes drinking seem the best way to have fun, turning weekdays into weekends. Messages that tie drinking to success, friendship and normalcy.

5. The bar room or cocktail party are places where grown-ups have fun, making drinking seem like a fine way of life.

6. It is okay to get drunk, some parents and their friends do. Nothing influences kids more.

7. Kids find that drinking helps with boredom and stress and smooths out the ups and downs of adolescence.

8. Kids think they are different. They feel drinking and doing drugs will do no personal harm and will cause no trouble. They feel indestructible.

9. For many poor city kids, using is a temporary escape from hopelessness.

...Your kids want to talk with you about alcohol and other drugs

The list could go on and on. There is plenty to make a young person say, "Who are you kidding," if he or she is told they are a bad person for drinking or smoking. More accurately, they are the victims of a society which places a premium on pleasure and self gratification. Your children should be made aware of this. Here, in our Western world, pain is often not suffered even slightly and there is a pill or potion for every minor physical or mental ailment.

Parents must take responsibility for breaking the hold alcohol and other drugs have on children. No greater reward can be imagined for so little time invested. If enough parents become involved, keeping kids drug free might even become an "in" thing to do!

Notes, Comments & Ideas

ALCOHOL: From Social Drinking To Addiction

I do not think anyone has yet come up with a better way of illustrating the progression of a drinking or drugging career as it moves toward the disease of chemical dependency than Dr. Vernon Johnson has with his Feeling Chart which is pictured and described in his classic book *I'll Quit Tomorrow*. I have used the Johnson Feeling Chart to illustrate what happens in the following mythical story. You will also find some words and phrases have been italicized. Use them as guide posts in recognizing the progression toward addiction.

Let me introduce John and his twin sister Mary. They are fifth graders in a public school situated just outside a large midwestern city. Their father is the owner of a machine shop, and their mother is a housewife who is heavily involved in volunteer work for their church. There are no other children in the family. If asked, the neighbors would describe them as quiet, industrious, and quite friendly. They seem to get on well together and with others in the community.

The twins are average students. Both are a bit shy and do not make friends easily. John has a paper route, and Mary already does some babysitting. Their father's business is only fair and currently suffers from cut backs in the defense industry; however, it provides for the family's needs with enough left over for his love of golf and for family vacations.

The mother is deeply religious. After her family, church takes up most of her time. She has a secret, which she is determined to keep from her husband and the twins — though she seems to drink normally, no one knows about her secret drinking.

Notes, Comments & Ideas

ALCOHOL: FROM SOCIAL DRINKING TO ADDICTION

She retrieves her bottle of vodka from the bottom of the dirty clothes hamper during the day and when she is alone. Her father had been an alcoholic and died from a heart attack at an early age. So far, she has been successful in hiding her problem and her tolerance for liquor is still high — she is able to drink 15 to 20 ounces of vodka a day without showing it.

To date, the children have not done any drinking or drugging. However, during the winter term, they were invited to a party at a classmate's house whose parents were away for the weekend.

Mary and John found the party in full swing when they arrived. Most of the kids were drinking soft drinks, though a few were working on cans of beer. After much urging by their host, John decided to try a beer. Mary declined and asked for an orange drink. When the beer was finished, John felt more at ease and less shy in such a large group. Before the party ended, John drank another beer. On the way home, he told Mary that she should drink some the next time because it made him feel great and the party was a whole lot more fun.

Let's take a look at how the Feeling Chart (next page) explains what happened. When the twins had arrived at the party, they were feeling nervous and apprehensive. They really did not want to be there. In fact, they felt more uncomfortable than many kids their age. Mary's mood did not change and she left the party feeling about the way she did when she arrived. John, on the other hand, said what a good time he had, and how he had talked with Mary's friend June, and how much fun it had all been.

Notes, Comments & Ideas

Figure 1		
PAIN	NORMAL	EUPHORIA
	A C B xxXxx	

On the Feeling Chart, here is what happened:

In Figure 1:

A. How John and Mary felt arriving at party and how Mary felt leaving the party.

B. How John felt after 2 beers.

C. How John felt leaving party and after effects of beer wear off. A good time to be remembered.

The beers John drank made him feel at ease, giving him self-confidence, so it was possible for him to talk with June quite easily. He had an excellent time all evening. As the effects of the beer wore off, he returned to feeling normal. And since so many of the other kids were drinking, John did not suffer from guilt or remorse.

The twins soon attended another party, and two important things happened: First, Mary, at John's urging, drank a beer, and besides being nauseated did not like the taste or the feeling of not quite being herself. Like many other teenagers, Mary's drinking career started and ended with the first drink. Secondly, ever since the first party, John had been *looking forward* to a can or so of beer and was pleased to *learn* the first can gave him the same feelings of pleasure he had experienced before. In fact, the evening became increasingly

Notes, Comments & Ideas

DEAR PARENTS PLEASE...

pleasant after John — on the theory that more is better — managed to down four beers in a short period of time:

Their effect on John was rather dramatic, changing this normally shy youngster into an extroverted, boisterous life of the party. On the way home, Mary remarked that he had not seemed himself and he looked foolish trying to dance with her friend June when he did not know how. John said he thought he had done very well and that she ought to try drinking again, because it made you feel so relaxed and happy. John is *learning* that *alcohol can be depended upon to bring forth the same good feelings time after time*. He awoke in the morning with a slight headache, otherwise none the worse for wear.

	──Figure 2──	
PAIN	NORMAL	EUPHORIA
	B	A
	xxXxxx	xxx

In Figure 2:

A. John after 4 quick beers feeling great, but not himself.

B. John next morning — headache, but no emotional pain.

Before getting up to get dressed for school, John lay back and thought with pleasure of the previous evening, the fun he had had, and in the same mood let his imagination go ahead to the next weekend and another party. It was to be at a cabin on the lake. No nosy grown-ups would be anywhere near, but he surely hoped June would be.

Notes, Comments & Ideas

...Your kids want to talk with you about alcohol and other drugs

Mary did not go this time. John, having told his parents he was going to a basketball game, went alone. He again enjoyed himself, but the next morning, in addition to a headache and queasy stomach, he had some feelings of guilt and remorse for having lied to his parents and for telling the boy whose parents owned the cabin that it was a dump. John had drunk six beers and had become rather obnoxious, loud-mouthed, and had used some off-color language. For the first time, the chart shows John paying for his actions with real emotional pain:

Figure 3

PAIN	NORMAL	EUPHORIA
B XX	XXXXXX	A XXXXX

In Figure 3:

A. John after 6 beers — out of control — obnoxious behavior.

B. John, next morning, besides a headache has remorse for lying and uneasiness about his behavior.

In thinking about the evening, John is soon able to *rationalize* his behavior on the basis that several of the other boys were obviously intoxicated and of course he was not as bad! (Hardly a reason to excuse his own behavior.)

Before long, John was hanging out with the group in school recognized as being far more interested in partying than studying.

John's way of life is changing and we see him three years later as he enters his freshman year of high school — he is a changed young man who *habitually drinks to get drunk*. And, as typical for those headed for trouble, he has developed *a high tolerance for alcohol* and is able to drink many of his companions "under the table." He *looks forward to drinking*, and if plans for a party are changed or canceled, John is upset, seeming moody and angry. John's grades have become marginal. Once a promising athlete, he shows no interest in making any team. His appearance has become sloppy and his parents continually nag him to get his hair cut.

Mary is worried about her brother. Out of love and loyalty for him, *she makes excuses and sometimes lies for him* when he is late or absent from school. John now drinks to get drunk as often as he can. Also, he has discovered marijuana, which is readily available. Smoking a joint before school, and perhaps one or two more during the day, helps John stay somewhat stoned on days when there is no chance to drink.

John also finds that pot and booze go together like peanut butter and jelly. Indeed, John is now chemically dependent and clearly, harmfully so. John would *deny* this and would say that he sees nothing wrong with things as they are. After all, he is not failing his courses and anyway, his parents and their friends drink all the time and besides, *he can quit anytime he wants*.

The fact is, John is now on the verge of becoming a full-blown addicted fifteen-year-old whose future prospects are in doubt. Some of the truth about his feelings can be described with the help of another Feeling Chart:

Notes, Comments & Ideas

PAIN	NORMAL	EUPHORIA
B		A
xxx	xxxxXxxxx	xxx

Figure 4

Figure 4:

A. John does not get quite the pleasure from drinking that he had been used to.

B. Besides painful hangovers, John is depressed much of the time and suffers from quilt and remorse because of his behavior.

The fact is, John can no longer control his drinking, and despite promising himself not to drink to drunkenness, he almost always does. Consequently, John now sometimes suffers from *blackouts,* and on awakening, cannot remember all that happened the night before. What he does remember is nearly always painful: fist-fights, arguments, unwelcome advances made on girls, foolish boasts and stupid lies. Gone are the days of feeling only a slight hangover. Now John feels depressed much of the time. It is only when he has a few drinks or smokes a joint that he feels normal. It is now unusual when alcohol or marijuana causes him to feel euphoric.

Time passes and John's life becomes a catastrophe. Despite his best intentions, he has lost control of his drinking. The time between disastrous episodes is becoming shorter and shorter. Each new failure to control his drinking makes it harder for John to look at what has happened to his life. For the most part, he *deludes himself* into thinking that there is nothing seriously wrong. The truth is, John is now a full-blown active alcoholic, *incapable of seeing himself as others do.* Occasionally, after some really horrible incident, John's denial system opens enough to give him a true look at what he has become. It is then that he is swamped by feelings of guilt, remorse, and self-loathing. He briefly realizes that his life is in shambles. The painfulness of these thoughts is overwhelming, so John quickly puts them out of his mind. By now, John's family knows something is terribly wrong; they vary from being worried and loving to being angry and nagging. Mary has spoken to him on many occasions and has finally been told to stop. John's grades are a disaster — last term he failed three courses and there is a good chance he will have to repeat his freshman year. His friends are the class trouble-makers whose behavior and attitudes seem specially designed to make their teachers' lives miserable.

—Figure 5—

PAIN	NORMAL	EUPHORIA
A ×××××	B ××××	

In Figure 5:

A. John's life has deteriorated to one of nearly continuous pain — both emotional and physical.

B. Drinking no longer produces feelings of euphoria. At best, alcohol can now only cause John to feel somewhat normal.

At this point there can be no doubt that John is squandering his adolescent years. If he lives to be an adult, he will become one with the emotional and intellectual maturity of a teenager and will be severely disadvantaged in a world where more and more jobs depend on brain power and advanced degrees.

Many would dismiss John as a bad kid who just didn't say "No" as Mrs. Reagan advised. The truth is he is a victim and a very sick one. Alcohol, not John, is the bad guy in this story. By inheritance, John acquired genes which made him susceptible to alcoholism. He received **no education or guidance from his parents** and was influenced by their drinking habits and those of his peers. He now is in desperate need of help, though he denies he is in any big trouble and still says he can quit any time. Had his parents known what to say, and had they started talking with him when he was 7 or 8, John's drinking and pot smoking might have never happened. Instead, ignorance has brought his parents to their wits end.

To make matters worse, John's mother is using his problem as an excuse to increase her drinking. John's sister, Mary, is devastated at what has happened to her brother. John's father has discovered his wife's hidden supply of vodka, which, added to John's problem, has caused him to spend frequent evenings away from home as an escape.

It's easy to see why alcoholism is called the *"family disease."* In John's family, no one knows what to do, and as the disease progresses, life for them becomes ever more difficult.

Notes, Comments & Ideas

Help came, but through tragedy. John suffered two broken legs, a broken arm, and a broken jaw when the car, in which he was a passenger, veered off the road and hit a tree. The sixteen year old driver was killed. That he was drunk was not in question, since an autopsy revealed the alcohol level in his blood was .20. It is miraculous John survived.

While hospitalized, he was fortunate to be treated by a physician who recognized John as an alcoholic. With the help of a specially trained addiction counselor, the doctor was able to convince John that his life had become unmanageable and was able to start him on the long hard road to recovery.

Sick as he was, this idea, at first, was horrifying to John. However, the trauma of the car crash, together with his already deeply troubled life was enough to cause his total surrender to the fact of his alcoholism. Months later, with the help of new young friends made at meetings of Alcoholics Anonymous, he was able to see a promising future in a life without alcohol or other drugs.

The essentials of John's story are the same for thousands upon thousands of children. Unfortunately, only a small percentage have such a positive ending. John's family was battered by his illness and their wounds need time to heal. This is complicated by his mother's drinking, but fortunately, as part of his hospital education, the concept of a family intervention had been discussed. After John told his father how it worked, he sought out John's hospital counselor, who coached the family to confront the mother with her

Notes, Comments & Ideas

behavior, so that she became willing to accept help.

John, like most youngsters whose alcoholism ran its course quickly, has done no great physical damage to himself. However, people who drink alcoholically for ten to 20 years can have devastating physical health problems. Alcohol's long term effect on the heart, liver, lungs, pancreas, and brain are clearly described in chapter six of Dr. James Milam and Katherine Ketcham's book, *Under the Influence*. Said to be the third largest killer after heart disease and cancer, alcohol problems account for about 25% of all general hospital admissions.

In deference to the feelings of the family of the patient, doctors often downplay alcohol in certifying the cause of death. For example: "Died from liver failure" is entered rather than "Died from cirrhosis of the liver due to acute alcoholism." Were the records accurate, alcoholism might move up to become the foremost killer of all.

While the disease is treatable, and victims can be recovered, only a small percentage now get help. Some say that only one out of 30 alcoholics recover and go on to live healthy, productive and sober lives.

The case for cutting demand through **education** has never been more compelling. And with children, **the earlier a parent starts the education process, the better the chance that family rules prohibiting use of alcohol/drugs will be successful.**

Notes, Comments & Ideas

In this, and preceding chapters, I have used alcohol to illustrate the "hows and whys" of misuse and addiction. These same principles apply to all misused drugs. Keep this in mind as you read the next few chapters which give you specific information on the most commonly misused drugs. You will need this information as you discuss each individual drug with your children.

DEAR PARENTS PLEASE...

Nicotine

From personal experience, I qualify as an expert on what the long term use of nicotine can do in raising havoc with your health. I am now an eleven year survivor of a heart attack which caused a two week hospital stay, including several days in the intensive care ward. When asked what caused the heart attack, my doctor did not hesitate a second before saying, "Smoking!" From all I have learned during my recovery, I am sure he was right. I wish now I had taken the warning labels on cigarettes seriously: "Smoking can be hazardous to your health." At no time, of course, did I think for a minute that the warning applied to me.

The government, through the superb work of Joseph Califano, then Secretary of Health, Education, and Welfare, and later, Surgeon General C. Everett Koop, has done a good job of taking much of the pleasure out of smoking. This government effort, to cut demand for cigarettes, is an example of how effective education and publicity can be. As any smoker knows, it is becoming more and more difficult to enjoy a cigarette with a clear conscience.

With an added spotlight on the harm second-hand smoke can cause, more adults are quitting for good, and fewer children start smoking careers. Overall, the figures are encouraging: around 30% of adults still smoke, instead of 75%, and for adolescents, the estimated percentage is 30 instead of 40. There is still a long way to go and according to the National Commission on Drug Free Schools, "Alcohol and tobacco create far greater risks to the health and safety of young people than all the other illicit drugs that one can name."

Notes, Comments & Ideas

NICOTINE

Notes, Comments & Ideas

So what is nicotine and how does it affect us? Nicotine is a minor stimulant found in tobacco. It can be smoked, sniffed or chewed. Continued use usually leads to addiction. When this happens, quitting is difficult and can cause severe physical and emotional pain, during an extended withdrawal period. Some say nicotine is harder to get off than heroin. Smokers usually become psychologically dependent before physical addiction sets in. Nicotine is a mood altering drug. Smoking often helps people get through difficult situations, either socially or at work. Nicotine use becomes a habit associated with various times of day, or the daily routine. The cigarette with coffee, with a drink, or after a meal are examples of when nicotine can become so satisfying.

Nowadays, almost everyone knows the long term use of nicotine is a leading cause of heart disease. It is the number one cause of lung cancer and emphysema. New findings about second-hand smoke are startling, to put it mildly. A recent study reported in the "New England Journal of Medicine" estimates children of smoking parents have twice the risk of developing lung cancer than those whose parents are non-smokers.

Talking with children about reasons not to smoke is certainly not easy. Kids are not impressed with possible heart or cancer troubles that may happen years down the road. They are also sure they can quit when it becomes necessary. It seems to me that to be successful, parents have no choice but to set an example by not smoking themselves. Otherwise, anything that is said will appear hypocritical.

...Your kids want to talk with you about alcohol and other drugs

Here are some suggestions which appeared in a recent FCD Educational Services "News Update" newsletter — I hope they will help:

What Can Parents Do?

1. Don't focus too much on long term health risks.

2. Reinforce the unattractiveness of smoking or using smokeless tobacco. (Research shows non-smoking teens are less interested in dating smokers.)

3. Emphasize the ugly aspects such as yellow teeth and bad breath.

4. Focus on the immediate damage to health such as shortness of breath, increased heart rate, coughing, damage to others through second hand smoke.

5. Appeal to their righteous indignation — young people are striving to gain independence and self control, talk to them about how the tobacco industry uses advertising to manipulate them into giving up control. Speak to the fact that nicotine addiction is a physical and psychological addiction. Mention the amount of control over their own lives they have given up to the drug. Again, remind them of the harm they are causing to others through secondary smoke released into the air.

6. Don't allow tobacco products or smoking in the house.

7. Encourage your child's school to forbid smoking — (Research has shown that school systems which allow smoking on school grounds graduate 25% more smokers per class than schools which don't).

Notes, Comments & Ideas

NICOTINE

8. Keep at it. It may be difficult for young people to go against the habits of their social group, especially if most of their peers smoke. Prevention is a process that takes place over time. Give young people bursts of information and concern from time to time and at times when they seem most receptive. To summarize, nicotine is an addictive, mood altering drug found in tobacco products. Smoking is responsible for over 300,000 deaths each year. This is several times more than for alcohol and all the other illicit drugs combined.

Notes, Comments & Ideas

DEAR PARENTS PLEASE...

Marijuana

MARIJUANA

A Few Street Names: Grass, Hemp, Joint, Reefer, Weed, Pot.

During the fall of 1977, I was invited by the head of a fine old school in Connecticut to give the FCD four-day alcohol education course to tenth graders. Things seemed to be going quite well until I was brought up short by a question from a young man, who asked, "What do you know about marijuana?" My reply was, "Nothing, what can you tell me?"

It turned out the students knew little more than I. They did agree pot was probably psychologically addictive but did not think it physically addictive. It did not take long for me to see that I had better get the facts on marijuana, because it was being used by a large percentage of the students in every school I visited.

Learning anything useful from the medical or scientific community was difficult, since very little had been published at the time. Dr. Gabriel Nahas, a professor of pharmacology at Columbia University in New York City, turned out to be a leading authority. I was able to obtain a copy of his fascinating book *Keep Off the Grass*, published by Reader's Digest Press in 1976. I paid Dr. Nahas a visit and came away convinced that, contrary to popular opinion, marijuana was an extremely dangerous drug. If used habitually, it could wreck the growing-up years. Tragically, kids who are chronic users often become immature and aimless young adults.

The history of Cannabis sativa (or marijuana, hashish, grass or pot) can be traced

Notes, Comments & Ideas

MARIJUANA

Notes, Comments & Ideas

back 4000 years when marijuana plants were grown in China for use as a sedative and as an all-purpose medication. Around 2000 B.C., priests in India boiled the leaves, stems, and flower tops into a potent liquid called bhang. Bhang was used before religious ceremonies and was described as a joy-giver, sky-flyer, and a soother of grief. It showed up next in the Middle East, and Muslims, for whom alcohol was prohibited, found hashish an excellent substitute which caused no pangs of conscience. Hashish, Arabic for grass, was first introduced in Egypt during the 13th century B.C., a time when that country was flourishing economically and culturally. Hash was first used by the well-to-do there, but eventually became the means by which peasants dulled the senses to their sad lot in life. Some historians have said that the slow decline of Egypt from a power in the region to a largely agrarian culture, was caused by the wide spread use of hashish.

Though marijuana or hashish use did not spread through Europe to any significant degree, it was used during the 19th century as a medication and was considered a wonder drug for people suffering from rabies, rheumatism, epilepsy and convulsions. American doctors soon were copying their European brethren, and such patent medicines as *"Tilden's Extract of Cannabis Sativa Indica"* were recommended for relief of a wide variety of diseases.

In 1910, marijuana was imported into Louisiana and Texas and was smoked in cigarette form by disadvantaged migrant workers as a relief from their sorry existence. It was discovered by early jazz

...Your kids want to talk with you about alcohol and other drugs

musicians in New Orleans who felt its intoxication enhanced their improvisational abilities.

Though marijuana use did spread north into some of the larger cities, there was not enough use to create a "drug problem." As the post World War II generation reached high school and college, marijuana came into its own. During the sixties, it was a staple for flower children, peaceniks, and protesters of the war in Vietnam.

Widespread use continues today and the supply is plentiful — home grown and imported. Marijuana is the third largest cash crop in California. Many would like to see it legalized; they cite its effectiveness as a pain killer for glaucoma and cancer patients. At FCD, we oppose legalization for several reasons. Two of the most important ones are:

1. Research into marijuana has a long way to go. It did not start until the 1970's but has already discovered things which may prove pot to be one of the most dangerous drugs of all.

2. We have seen it ruin the adolescent years of too many bright kids, causing them to be immature, unmotivated young adults, who, if they stop using, face years of abstinence before their recovery is complete and they are able to function to their full potential.

The following story was written by an ex-member of the FCD teaching staff and first appeared in our newsletter for schools:

Students often tell me that marijuana is safer than alcohol because there is no hangover and "It's not physically addicting." Yet, in every school I teach, several students tell me they

Notes, Comments & Ideas

MARIJUANA

would like to stop smoking pot but are unable to. Others tell me they have tried to cut down but have had little success.

I smoked marijuana for eight years; during six of those years I smoked daily. One of the most significant events to occur in those eight years of pot smoking (and other miscellaneous drug use) was to have a friend tell me I was "hooked on pot." I laughed and told him it was impossible to get hooked on pot because it wasn't physically addicting. My friend, who is a recovering alcoholic, said it appeared to him that I smoked pot like he used to drink. He suggested that if I wasn't hooked I should be able to stop using for a while without any trouble. If I chose to resume smoking pot later, I would at least have established that I had the choice.

It sounded reasonable to me. I asked him how long a time would be necessary in order to clearly know if I was hooked or exercising a preference? I was hoping he would say "two weeks," (My fear was that he would say six weeks or more, which seemed likely to be an uncomfortable amount of time). He suggested I abstain for six months! He might just as well have said six years. I couldn't imagine why anyone would want to go for six months without getting stoned. Wouldn't a couple of weeks be enough to prove the point? He suggested that I attend a meeting of Alcoholics Anonymous with him to stimulate my thinking on the matter.

I went to an A.A. meeting with my friend and listened to people talk of how they had ruined their lives with alcohol and other drugs. But my life wasn't ruined! I was married, working and supposedly happy. I had friends and hobbies, and I wasn't physically addicted. Then, one of the speakers at the meeting talked

Notes, Comments & Ideas

...Your kids want to talk with you about alcohol and other drugs

about the fourth step of A.A.'s twelve suggested steps in recovery:

"Make a searching and fearless moral inventory of yourself." This impressed me. For several weeks after the meeting I considered how self scrutiny had been missing from my life. I began to watch myself smoking marijuana. I smoked every day, usually in the late afternoon or evening. While I never got stoned at work, occasionally I would smoke during lunch break. On weekends I smoked in the morning, afternoon and evening. I smoked when I went to the movies, while watching T.V., while listening to music, when riding my bike, when driving to the store (yes, driving under the influence — but it was O.K. — I was more relaxed driving stoned), and especially prior to going out to dinner. Some people would have labeled that amount of use a "drug dependence." My friend called it "being hooked." Whichever, I began to consider it somewhat excessive.

So I decided to cut down. I would smoke pot only at night; maybe on the weekends; just one joint on weekday nights; only two joints per day; only if someone offered it to me; only before going to bed, only . . . I couldn't do it. For the first time in my life I realized I was not in control of my marijuana use. This was a very upsetting revelation, and to calm myself I smoked a little more. But this business of a "searching and fearless moral inventory" kept haunting me. It became increasingly obvious that I had to look more closely at my life.

My career was at a standstill, I felt flat and unmotivated. There were issues in my marriage I couldn't face or deal with honestly, and several other relationships were in turmoil. I had developed an ulcer which eventually landed me in the hospital. Marijuana use was

Notes, Comments & Ideas

MARIJUANA

helping me avoid the pain of working on myself and my relationships — but at least I wasn't physically addicted — I was just "hooked."

Many of the students I work with today are astounded to hear that it took me three years from the time I admitted to being hooked until I was finally able to stop smoking pot. That's three years of therapy (unstoned), meditation and relaxation classes, and a rebirth of spiritual values through group meetings and individual work — hard work! These young people ask me if I can't smoke a joint just once in a while and I tell them no, not even a single puff. I tell them there was nothing I received from drug use that compares with how good I feel today without drug use. Becoming drug free helped me become healthy — staying drug free makes me able to do things that keep me healthy.

I ask students if they know someone who needs to stop smoking pot but doesn't; someone who wants to stop but can't. More than half say they know someone at risk in just this way — "an individual who doesn't want to accept it, since marijuana isn't physically addicting."

There is much about marijuana that is not known. It is a complicated drug. It is made up of at least 421 different chemicals known as cannabinoids of which the most important is THC, (Delta — 9 tetrahydro cannabinol). THC is the main psychoactive ingredient and can be five to ten percent of the total content — which is a big increase from only a few years ago. A fair amount is now known about THC, though there is still much to be learned. Little or nothing is known about many of the other cannabinoids.

Notes, Comments & Ideas

THC is *fat* soluble and, unlike drugs that are *water* soluble like alcohol, it remains in the body much longer. A person smoking a joint today might test positive for traces of THC three weeks from now. It is important to understand that THC gets into every part of the body, does not leave quickly and affects *all* of the most vital parts:

The lungs — Marijuana is damaging to the lungs — (several times more so than cigarettes) and extended use can be an important factor in causing lung cancer and other diseases, such as bronchitis and emphysema.

The brain — Research on pot's effect on the brain has been quite extensive. Though more is needed, some conclusions can be drawn:

> Marijuana affects memory and learning. Information stored in the brain when cramming for an exam often cannot be recalled properly if sufficient amounts of THC are present in the brain cells, so they do not function properly.

> Reading comprehension and speaking skills are effected. No wonder the grades of habitual smokers can be so poor.

> Driving while high can be as bad as driving drunk — the driver's reaction time and ability to track properly is out of whack; therefore, the danger of a disastrous collision is multiplied.

Reproductive system — Of real concern to researchers of late is the effects of THC on the complex system of glands and hormones that oversee and regulate growth and sexual development.

This is particularly worrisome as the age of children using marijuana has become so much younger. Again, more research is needed, but it appears THC lowers the testosterone levels in males and also causes the levels of two key hormones to drop in females which has caused problems of ovulation and menstruation. While this whole area is open to question, it, in itself, provides a fairly compelling reason for not using marijuana.

The immune system — is affected because continued use of marijuana causes a decrease in the manufacture of white blood cells that are crucial in warding off infections such as bronchitis and many other viruses. This makes one wonder if marijuana is appropriate for medicinal use except in terminal cases.

Amotivation Syndrome — is a term that has come to be used to generally describe the changes long term use of marijuana causes in the way users think, feel, and behave. Chronic use provides an escape from the normal stress and adolescent pain of growing up. The young user often becomes withdrawn and does not participate in school activities such as sports. The young user may be full of good intentions and easy talk of future feats, nothing seems to get done as the school years speed by. Here again is a way of producing an emotionally and intellectually crippled young adult.

The following is a list which may be helpful in spotting the chronic marijuana user:

1. Transition from active participation in, to passive withdrawal from, normal interests.

Notes, Comments & Ideas

2. Decline in the quality of work at school.

3. Alienation from family; antisocial behavior and lack of consideration for the feelings of others.

4. Chronic redness of eyes.

5. Neglect of personal hygiene and general appearance.

6. Paranoia, defensiveness, and touchiness with respect to restrictions and mild criticisms.

7. Neglect of chores or other responsibilities.

8. Noticeable weight loss.

9. Mysterious telephone calls. Secretiveness concerning new friends.

10. Unwillingness to talk about money spent, including the disappearance of money and other valuables from the home or workplace.

Bear in mind that these clues can all indicate other problems and are not necessarily drug related. But it is important at least to consider them when dealing with troubled young people.

To sum up, please take marijuana very seriously. It is a complicated drug about which not much is known. It *is* clear that THC, the active ingredient, can cause a wide variety of physical and mental health problems. There is ample cause for a parent to prohibit pot use, beside the fact that it is an illegal drug.

Notes, Comments & Ideas

MARIJUANA

I am sure many of today's parents hold to the idea that marijuana is not harmful if used by adults occasionally and moderately. Perhaps based on the incomplete research on pot's extraordinarily complex makeup it is not possible to refute this. However, I do think parents make a huge mistake smoking around their growing children. I remember several years ago reading what a tenth grader in a New England boarding school wrote about the FCD visit, "I got a lot out of the FCD course and what you had to say about smoking pot was kind of scary. I'm going to cut way back but I don't see any harm in smoking a joint with mom when I go home? Do you?" Enough already; you be the judge!

Notes, Comments & Ideas

DEAR PARENTS PLEASE...

Other Drugs

STIMULANTS

COCAINE AND CRACK

A Few Street Names: *Blow, C., Coke, Flake, Nose Candy, Toot.*

> *"Cocaine Bill and Morphine Sue walking arm and arm down the Avenue, come on, my honey, have a (sniff) on me, Have a (sniff) on me."*

There is a lot more to this song that we sometimes sang at college drinking parties in the early thirties. If cocaine was causing any significant problems then, we did not know it. From the standpoint of damage to the health of the heavy user, it is interesting that cocaine's devastating effects on the physical, emotional and spiritual well being have only recently become understood. It is tremendously important that parents understand all the problems this drug can create for their children.

While the use of cocaine is many times less than either alcohol, nicotine, or marijuana, there is another side to its use which often makes me think cocaine is, in some ways, the worst drug of all — corruption and violent crime follow wherever it goes, from the coca plantations, along the smuggler's routes, to dealers in both quiet, rural communities as well as the inner cities. Cocaine and crack cocaine trafficking is at the root of many of the murders and shootings which make life in our cities so difficult, particularly for the disadvantaged who have no choice but to stay there.

Shutting down the cocaine traffic is enormously difficult, as proven by the government's largely unsuccessful

Notes, Comments & Ideas

STIMULANTS — COCAINE AND CRACK

"War on Drugs." There is so much money to be made all along the distribution routes that profit always outweighs risk. There is also no lack of eager replacements to fill the shoes of those who are busted. Perhaps many more policemen on inner city streets are the best hope to control the violence that is now so rampant.

Historically, almost everyone knows that cocaine comes from leaves of the coca plant. These were chewed in early times by the native South American tribes. The Spanish conquistadors allowed the habit to go on after conquering much of the area because they found they got more work from the natives who chewed than from those who didn't.

During the 1800's cocaine, the active ingredient of the coca leaf, was isolated in pure form. It wasn't long before cocaine was introduced into a wide range of medical products — patent medicines, syrups, nasal sprays, also into cigars, cigarettes and liquors. In 1888, Dr. J.C. Pemberton introduced a five-cent drink called Coca-Cola, which he touted as an antidote for headaches and fatigue. Dr. Sigmund Freud recommended cocaine in the treatment of nervousness and morphine addiction.

In 1906 the Pure Food and Drug Act required that all medicines containing cocaine be so labeled. In 1914 the Harrisson Narcotic Act prohibited non-medical use of the drug in the U.S. From then until the late seventies illicit use of cocaine was not a large problem, but as a drug for the roaring 80's, cocaine seemed ideal. In a time of excesses, cocaine use seemed a great way to boost performance

Notes, Comments & Ideas

...Your kids want to talk with you about alcohol and other drugs

STIMULANTS – COCAINE AND CRACK

and to feel turned on and revved up. During this period cocaine was, at first, thought to be fairly harmless. Before long, evidence began to pick up which makes it appear that — when the whole story is in — the scientific community may brand cocaine as one of the most dangerous and highly addictive drugs around.

Cocaine is both a stimulant which works on the central nervous system and an anesthetic that numbs any tissue it touches. It blocks both fatigue and appetite. It is mostly sold as a white crystal-like powder and can be used in several ways — snorted from spoons or straw-like devices, or a more intense high can be achieved by injection or using the newer smokable form.

Physical problems are common with long term use: heart attacks from damaged tissue and abnormal heartbeats, strokes caused from heightened blood pressure levels, gradual weight loss, malnutrition and "burn out." Of course, you can get into trouble the first time you use cocaine by overdosing and putting yourself into a coma which can be fatal.

Psychologically, cocaine use is a joy ride which brings on feelings of intense euphoria followed by severe depression as the rush wears off. This is often coupled with an overpowering craving for more. Researchers have come to rank cocaine at the top of the list of highly addictive drugs. Long term use eventually creates extreme paranoia, hallucinations and bizarre compulsive behavior. Cocaine dependency can be defeated, but it's not easy. Many ex-users say that they got many times more grief than pleasure.

Notes, Comments & Ideas

CRACK

A Few Street Names: *Super White, White Cloud, Cloud 9, Serpico.*

Crack is an inexpensive highly addictive form of cocaine. When it showed up a few years ago, cocaine use took a giant step forward. As crack spread throughout the country, it caused large increases in the number of users and the number of users who became addicted. It has also caused a huge increase in street crime both in the cities and in the countryside.

Crack is cocaine mixed with water and baking soda. When the water dries, the mixture is cut into pellet size "rocks" which, for as little as $10, will provide several brief incredibly intense rushes. Since crack is smoked it reaches the brain in a few seconds creating intense feelings of euphoria. A few minutes after coming down, even the neophyte user experiences an overwhelming desire for more. In general, troubles from habitual crack use are much the same as with regular cocaine, although some effects are intensified because crack is smoked.

Because it's so easy to come by and so inexpensive, crack has become the fastest growing drug around. Its use by young people has spawned an epidemic of drug related street crime. Even the newspapers published in country towns contain stories of murder, assault, or other kinds of cocaine or crack related mayhem.

Notes, Comments & Ideas

STIMULANTS — AMPHETAMINES

AMPHETAMINES

Notes, Comments & Ideas

A Few Street Names: *Uppers, Bennies, Cross Tops, Black Beauties, Speed, Bumblebees, Pep Pills, Ludies.*

Amphetamines, dextroamphetamines and methamphetamines are closely related drugs which stimulate the central nervous system and create feelings of alertness and, in general, speed up the physical activity of the user. From a medical standpoint, amphetamines have limited uses today and are usually restricted to treating narcolepsy (a rather rare disorder typified by a periodic, uncontrollable need to sleep) or for short term use as an appetite suppressant and weight loss agent.
The brand names for amphetamine-like prescription drugs include Benzedrine, Dexedrine, Preludine and Biphetamine.

Amphetamines have been around for a long time. They were first synthesized during the 19th Century, but did not become popular in the U.S. until the 1930's and 40's when pharmaceutical companies became enthusiastic about their stimulant qualities and touted them as the latest thing in miracle drugs. During the 50's and 60's they were prescribed for a whole range of problems including fatigue, listlessness, and depression. They really came into their own as diet pills during the 60's and early 70's to satisfy American obsession with thinness. When use peaked in 1971 several billion pills were gulped down yearly in the name of being fashionably thin.

It rather quickly became obvious that amphetamines were creating all kinds of unforeseen health problems including psychological dependency plus feelings of anxiety, huge mood swings, panic and

DEAR PARENTS PLEASE...

STIMULANTS —AMPHETAMINES

hallucinations and paranoia. Some long term users became convinced they were being victimized for irrational and ridiculous reasons.

When the legitimate amphetamine manufacturers ceased production, they were replaced by suppliers who provided illegal substitutes for sale by street dealers. Besides an assortment of "look alike" speed or crank pills they also sell crystal, a super-charged form of speed made of methamphetamine. Crystal is highly addictive and can be injected, smoked, or taken orally. Symptoms include those already described with "regular" amphetamine use but are often more severe. Street names include ice, super ice, glass, LA Glass and LA Crystal. The exhilarating "rush" provided by these drugs is more than offset by the psychological and physical damage that occurs through long term use.

Long term users of amphetamines can become paranoid, distrustful and suspicious of others. They have unreasonable feelings that everyone they meet is determined to make their lives as difficult as possible. These persecution complexes are particularly distressing to their friends and families. It has been said that using amphetamines and their closely related drug cousins is one of the most effective ways to accelerate wear and tear on the human system. Not unlike taking the elasticity out of a rubber band.

While kids do not use amphetamines to the extent they do alcohol, nicotine or marijuana, parents should be aware that some of the most popular varieties are of unknown origin and contain unknown ingredients.

Notes, Comments & Ideas

...Your kids want to talk with you about alcohol and other drugs

STIMULANTS —AMPHETAMINES • HALLUCINOGENS —LSD

If you want to know more about amphetamines read *The Facts About Drug Use* by Dr. Barry Stimmel. You will find a fascinating history of amphetamine use over the years and a full description of the danger of misusing these drugs.

HALLUCINOGENS

LSD (LYSERGIC ACID DIETHYLAMIDE)

A Few Street Names: *Acid, Blotter, Blue Dots, Zigzag.*

A few years ago it appeared that the use of LSD by college and high school students was declining. There were sighs of relief, as this drug can be a killer. Unfortunately, it has been making a comeback, and is even showing up in middle schools and occasionally in elementary schools.

LSD was discovered in the 1940's by a Swiss chemist named Hoffman. It made its debut in the United States in the 1960's. Timothy Leary, a Harvard lecturer, was an early LSD guru and did much to promote it as a shortcut to new insights and spiritual experiences. It was a favorite drug for many of the "turn on, tune in, and drop out" generation. The dosage level was higher in those days. Today it is rare to hear of tragedies such as a kid, high on a trip, jumping from a window because he thought he was a bird; or a girl swimming away from the shore until she drowned. The young today use LSD for visual stimulation, entertainment, and simply to get high. They do not consider it to be particularly dangerous, which is just not so.

Notes, Comments & Ideas

HALLUCINOGENS —LSD

Emergency room cases and LSD related arrests are on the increase and there is no sign that this trend will stop any time soon.

Getting high on LSD today is easy. The price of a dose on the street varies from $2 to $5, and the supply is quite plentiful. Unlike either marijuana or alcohol, there is no smell and since it comes absorbed by blotting paper or as a pill, it is easy to hide and carry.

What kids do not know is that an LSD trip can last as long as eighteen hours and can cause visual and auditory hallucinations which can reoccur months or even years later. These "flashbacks" are unnerving to say the least.

A trip can go wrong, causing acute psychosis and a breakdown from reality. Symptoms and behavior often appear to be like those of someone suffering from schizophrenia.

As with many drugs sold on the street, the purity of LSD is always in doubt. The work of the underground chemist cannot be trusted. Furthermore, it is so powerful that a dose is measured in micrograms (millionths of a gram). About 30 micrograms is mildly psychoactive. Currently, between 50 and 150 micrograms are found in an average dose.

For a time, LSD was thought to be the perfect answer for anyone wishing to gain an understanding of his or her ultimate self. Indeed it does produce profound changes in the way one thinks, feels, and perceives the world; however, there is always the possibility of a "bad trip." This can cause panic and anxiety so severe that hospital care and ongoing psychiatric counseling is needed.

Notes, Comments & Ideas

...Your kids want to talk with you about alcohol and other drugs

HALLUCINOGENS —LSD

An associate who took LSD at age 16 has kindly provided a description of his experiences in the form of a letter to a friend:

April, 1976

Dear Kim,

Charlie, Susan, Rick and I stayed out all night and we each took a hit of LSD and flipped out. Susan just met Rick, but she kept calling him Craig, so we all started to call him Craig. He kept saying, "Please, call me Craig" if we called him Rick. I dropped the fire off my cigarette and each spark turned into millions and more and more and more. The whole sky was swishing around and moving and stars were multi-colored. Charlie went down to this pond we parked near to scare the ducks and when he came back up to the car, I saw him as a gigantic spider, which turned into policemen.

I thought Charlie was a policeman and the spider's legs turned into police and Charlie became the chief and Susan, Craig and I were going to be busted. It was like they (the imaginary police) were shining a big spotlight on us. We were like, in a movie or on T.V. news about flipped-out acid heads. Craig was acting like it was true just to flip me out and I started to wave my arms in front of me. It seemed like we were all huddled together (but we weren't) and yelling "No, no, no, please God no." I almost passed out. Then Craig said, "It's all right and I said, "Craig, I'm falling in cow pies." But, we were in a graveyard and there are no cow pies in a graveyard...At least not in that one.

I am sure you will put LSD high on the list of drugs with which no child should experiment.

Notes, Comments & Ideas

HALLUCINOGENS —LSD • PCP

LSD was classified as a Schedule I drug in the 1970's along with other very dangerous drugs such as heroin.

PCP (PHENCYCLIDINE)

A Few Street Names: *Angel Dust, Hog, Peace Pill.*

PCP is classified as a hallucinogen and has had a checkered history. It has been known by many aliases. Though not widely used, your children should be taught about it because it can cause violent physical reactions and, at worst, turn the user into a suicidal or homicidal maniac.

PCP was developed as an anesthetic after WWI but was not much used until 1957 when the Parke-Davis Co. brought it to market and named it Sernyl.

Sernyl worked quite well as a surgical anesthesia, but was taken off the market because patients often suffered from hallucinations, delirium, jumbled speech or hyper-excitability.

Later, Parke-Davis brought PCP to the market again as an animal tranquilizer named Sernylin.

As a recreational drug, word had spread that PCP was indeed bad news and responsible for numerous ugly trips. But street dealers were quick to envision other highly profitable uses for it. PCP became a raw material added to batches of marijuana, heroin and LSD.

PCP has piled up many aliases, and like the cat, has many lives. In the mid-1970's, it picked up popularity and again gained bad press, because too many who used it became drug-crazed murderers, rapists, or robbers.

Notes, Comments & Ideas

...Your kids want to talk with you about alcohol and other drugs

HALLUCINOGENS — PCP

In 1978 the U. S. Government imposed new controls over the use of Sernylin, which caused Parke-Davis to finally get out of manufacturing and marketing PCP as an animal tranquilizer, or anything else. Unfortunately, it is still sold on the streets, disguised as a number of other drugs. The most common form is smokable — drug-laced cigarettes or parsley joints.

Use produces a bizarre mixture of effects. PCP acts as an anesthetic, stimulant, depressant, and hallucinogen at the same time. Of all the drugs, PCP is the one best known for its unpredictability. There is often a sense of physical and psychological detachment. Time and space become muddled. Vivid hallucinations often occur and the initial feelings of euphoria fade into withdrawal and isolation. A low dose trip — three to eight milligrams — often appears as a mild high. Slurred speech is a common side effect. It usually lasts about half a day.

With higher doses — 12 milligrams and above — a trip can last several days. These can be fearful experiences with vivid and terrifying hallucinations, rapid and uncontrollable mood swings, and outbursts of violent aggressive behavior. Users can lose all sense of space and time and may accidentally injure themselves or others.

It seems incredible that PCP is still around. Unfortunately, people are willing to give it a try, despite its universally bad reputation.

Notes, Comments & Ideas

MESCALINE / PEYOTE

A Few Street Names: *Buttons, Beans, Cactus, Mescal.*

The peyote cactus has a small crown and a long root. The crown is cut off and dried to form a brownish disc, which is known as a "button." Peyote buttons were used by Mexican Indians centuries ago as a hallucinogenic sacrament in part of their worship of the deities. It was also believed that the peyote button was a powerful medicine that could cure many illnesses.

During the nineteenth century, use of peyote spread to many North American Indian tribes and took the place of the more dangerous "red bean," which was then commonly used as a religious sacrament.

A peyote trip produces many of the effects of LSD — sensations of weightlessness, visual distortions and hallucinations. The taste of peyote buttons is disagreeable and before the trip kicks in, vomiting often occurs. This was viewed as an act of purification by the Indians.

Mescaline is the main psychoactive ingredient of the peyote button. It was synthesized by a German scientist in 1898 and for the next few decades psychiatrists used it as a medicine in the experimental treatment of alcoholism and neuroses. Mescaline is also found in one other species of North American cactus. It is called the San Pedro cactus and is not related to the peyote cactus. In milder form, it produces the same reactions and is similar to peyote in most respects.

Notes, Comments & Ideas

HALLUCINOGENS —MESCALINE / PEYOTE • MDMA

In many instances there have been reports that long term use can cause a variety of physical and mental health problems. Symptoms include flashbacks, convulsions and neurosis.

MDMA (Phenylisopropylmines)

A Few Street Names: *Ecstasy, X, Adam.*

MDMA/ecstasy was synthesized in Germany early in the twentieth century. It is a psychoactive drug which came into wide use by therapists in the 1970's. It was thought by some psychotherapists that its use as a medicine could, in a few hours, produce the same benefits as years of therapy. It was also used experimentally in the treatment of certain addictions, including alcohol.

Interestingly, MDMA/ecstasy is a psychoactive drug, phenylisopropylmine, which makes it a cousin of methamphetamine or speed.

Ecstasy quickly became a favorite of people who wanted to feel its rush and ecstatic high in a party situation. In the early 1980s, it was the drug of choice by many yuppies who believed it could help them be more aware of themselves and gain higher insights into the whys and wherefores of life.

In 1984, MDMA/ecstasy was placed on schedule one of the Controlled Substance Act, putting it in the same league as heroin, LSD, and cocaine. It is illegal to produce, distribute, or possess this chemical, so now it comes from underground labs. There is no way of knowing what is in ecstasy when it hits the streets.

Notes, Comments & Ideas

HALLUCINOGENS —MDMA • PSYLOCIBIN

Accepted scientific knowledge about the long term effects of MDMA/ecstasy is very sketchy. It is suspected that it may cause damage to the neurotransmitter system of the brain, but more research is needed. Nausea, vomiting, fluctuations in blood pressure and heart rate, blurred vision, and tension in the jaw and facial muscles have all been observed as part of an MDMA/ecstasy trip.

Rather than making the user kinder and gentler, the opposite may occur. He or she may act and talk aggressively and is apt to hog the conversation in an unpleasant manner. Based on what is known today, it is hard to dream up any good reason to take the risk of even experimenting with an illegal, potentially harmful drug like MDMA/ecstasy.

PSILOCYBIN

A Few Street Names — *Shrooms, Magic Mushrooms, Silly Putty.*

Found in a variety of Mexican and American mushrooms, psilocybin acts much like LSD except effects are milder. When eaten, reaction kicks in after about 30 minutes and lasts for several hours. In synthetic form, it appears as a white powder.

Among the negative feelings it can cause are anxiety, nervousness, nausea, stomach pains and shivering.

Notes, Comments & Ideas

...Your kids want to talk with you about alcohol and other drugs

NARCOTICS

OPIATES

Opiates are a group of drugs which are used medically to relieve pain. When misused, they have a high potential to create dependency and addiction. Some opiates come from the resin of the Asian poppy. These include: opium, morphine, heroin and codeine. Others, such as neperidine (demerol), are manufactured synthetically.

As pain relievers, the opiates are tremendously helpful. I remember a skiing accident over 40 years ago, as though it were yesterday. Skiing a new trail not officially opened, I had managed to hit a stump which caused me to somersault and stop short against a snow covered boulder. When I finally arrived at a New Hampshire hospital (via ski patrol toboggan and a hearse doubling as an ambulance), the pain was made bearable by an injection of morphine into my blood stream.

I do not remember how many ribs were broken, but I know that most were. I also had a badly bruised kidney. I do remember the pain being excruciating, and the memory of relief brought by the morphine is just as clear.

During the first ten days of recovery, morphine was prescribed in gradually decreasing amounts. The doctor was concerned that I would become addicted. There is no disagreement that opiates are highly addictive.

Of the opiates, heroin is the most misused as an illegal pleasure drug. Perhaps 90% of all narcotic users choose heroin; however,

Notes, Comments & Ideas

there is also some illicit use of medicinal narcotics, including paregoric, which contains opium, and cough syrup containing codeine, morphine and meperidine.

HEROIN

A Few Street Names — *Junk, Smack, Snow, Horse.*

Heroin is sold as a white or brownish powder which is usually dissolved in water and injected. A great deal of heroin sold on the streets is diluted, or "cut" with other substances, like sugar or quinine.

At first, heroin produces a rush and then feelings of euphoria. The effects can last several hours. It is highly addictive, and anyone using it regularly becomes dependent.

Acquiring an adequate supply often becomes the centerpiece of an addict's life. This frequently leads to a life of crime which produces prison confinement for a large percentage of users. The heroin addict runs many other risks — unsterile needles are a leading cause of the spread of AIDS, tetanus and serum hepatitis. Another risk is not knowing the consistency of the dose being injected which can lead to overdose and death. Long term users may develop infections of the heart lining and skin abscesses.

Many heroin addicts wishing to break their habit seek help from methadone clinics. Methadone is a synthetic or manufactured drug which prevents the painful withdrawal symptoms suffered by the heroin addict and stops the intense craving for a fix. Critics of the methadone solution say it merely substitutes one drug

Notes, Comments & Ideas

NARCOICS —HEROIN

for another and is not a cure. Daily visits to the clinic for the prescribed amount are necessary. Some individuals on methadone maintenance receive counseling and eventually recover from all drug abuse.

As if heroin wasn't causing enough trouble, it has recently showed up in a smokable form and at quite an affordable cost. This of course eliminates fear of contracting AIDS from dirty needles. Some say heroin will be to the 90's as cocaine was to the 80's. Let's hope they are wrong!

Dr. Barry Stimmel in his excellent book *The Facts About Drug Use* has fully described the consequences of using heroin and the other opiates. For those wanting more information, Dr. Stimmel's account is must reading.

Notes, Comments & Ideas

SEDATIVES AND HYPNOTICS

A Few Street Names: *Barbs, Green Dragons, Yellow Jackets, Red Birds.*

This is a large grouping of drugs which act on the central nervous system as depressants. They are commonly known as downers. Most sedatives and hypnotics fit into two main categories: the barbiturates and the benzodiazepines. Methaqualone is a popular drug that does not fit in either category.

BARBITURATES

The barbiturates include phenobarbital, nembutal and seconal, which are commonly prescribed for sleeping problems.

A large percentage of drug related deaths is caused by overdosing on the barbiturates or by combining them with alcohol. The potential for an overdose is higher because tolerance comes quickly and increasing amounts are needed for the desired effect. Dependency is easily achieved, and withdrawal is a painful and lengthy process, often including hallucinations and seizures. Troubles stemming from barbiturates are mostly caused by the misuse and overdosing of medical prescriptions.

BENZODIAZEPINES

Benzodiazepines include the widely prescribed tranquilizers Valium and Librium, along with the less used, more powerful drugs such as Thorazine, Mellanil and Halcion. For symptoms of anxiety, stress, tension, or nervousness, Valium is the favorite drug of all. It is easy to become hooked on it, and because Valium is *fat* soluble, withdrawal is usually long and painful.

Notes, Comments & Ideas

SEDATIVES AND HYPNOTICS —BENZODIAPINES • METHAQUALONE

A recovered alcoholic friend of mine told me how she had become dependent on Valium while trying to kick alcohol addiction. Recognizing this new problem, she became determined to rid herself of it. She soon found herself entering an extremely painful world filled with depression, anxiety, agitation and sleeplessness. Only with the help of several good friends was she able to struggle through this extended period of severe pain.

Librium is another common tranquilizer. At alcohol treatment centers, it is often used effectively to prevent patients from going into delirium tremens or convulsions. By curbing feelings of anxiety and agitation, it makes a painful four or five days of alcohol withdrawal safer and easier to bear. Since Librium itself is highly addictive, its use is stopped as soon as the acute withdrawal phase is over.

People for whom such drugs as Valium and Librium have been prescribed should beware of combining them with alcohol. In that combination, one plus one hardly ever equals two. More likely, it equals four or six, depending on the individual. In fact, according to the National Academy of Sciences, a good number of deaths have been reported following the simultaneous use of alcohol and tranquilizers like Valium or Ativan.

METHAQUALONE

A Few Street Names: *Ludes, Sopers, 714s.*

Methaqualone, is a favorite "downer" with many people. It was first introduced in the U.S. in 1965 and was hailed as a substitute for dangerous barbiturates since it was thought be non-addictive and free from side effects.

SEDATIVES AND HYPNOTICS —METHAQUALONE

Unfortunately, this turned out to be untrue, and one by one the manufacturers of such drugs as Quaaludes, Soper, Optimil and Somnafal, took their products off the market.

Not surprisingly, there is a large, illegal underground market in existence today. The imports of illegal methaqualone tablets and powder exceed 100 tons a year. As with other drugs sold illegally on the street, there is no way to know the true identity of the ingredients.

In many ways, methaqualone creates the same effect as alcohol. The drug works on the central nervous system and initially breaks down inhibitions and creates feelings of euphoria, confidence and wisdom. However, as these effects wear off, depression sets in, which is usually more severe than one induced by alcohol.

It is easy to build a tolerance to methaqualone. As larger and larger amounts are needed to get high, the danger of a fatal overdose increases.

A last warning: use of the sedative-hypnotic drugs should be strictly limited to the instructions accompanying the physicians prescription. Otherwise, they can be extremely dangerous trouble makers.

Notes, Comments & Ideas

INHALANTS —GLUES, SOLVENTS, AEROSOLS • NITROUS OXIDE

INHALANTS

Notes, Comments & Ideas

Since large numbers of very young children start their first experimenting with some of these drugs, parents need to understand that they too can cause lots of trouble and are best left alone.

GLUES, SOLVENTS AND AEROSOLS

Glues, solvents and aerosols are cheap and easy to come by. When inhaled, they cause a quick, short-lived high which in some ways resembles the feelings of giddiness and intoxication achieved by misusing alcohol. Examples of the most commonly sniffed are:

•Glue •Cleaning solution •Nail polish remover •Paints and paint remover •Butane •Fabric guard •Liquid paper whitener •Typewriter cleaning fluid

Freon gas, methanol, naptha, and carbon tetrachloride are key ingredients used in these substances. They are so popular that they are used by an estimated 30 percent of all our youngsters. Most do not use them for more than a year or so. But it is important to remember that there are real dangers connected with even occasional use. A substantial dose can produce hallucinations, panic attacks, wild mood swings and a state of confusion. Chronic use may cause liver, kidney, lung or brain damage. A single very high dose can result in such a severe toxic shock that hospital care is needed. In some cases, use of inhalants has been fatal.

NITROUS OXIDE

Nitrous oxide has a long medical history as an anesthetic. It is widely used in oral surgery and other dental work. It is popu-

INHALANTS —NITROUS OXIDE •AMYL NITRITE

larly known as "giggle gas" and is a favorite intoxicant of high school and college students.

Laughing gas is easily obtained. For example, it is the propellant in whipped cream canisters and can be obtained from mail order houses under the name of Whippets. Each "Whippet" produces one or two blasts of nitrous oxide, which creates feelings of giddiness and dreaming or floating sensations.

Not a great deal of research has been done on the long term dangers of using nitrous oxide as a recreational drug. There is concern that damage to the lungs and blood vessels may occur through the increased pressure which comes from the gas as it enters the user's body.

NITRITES

Amyl nitrite was introduced in the mid 1800's as a medicine to relieve the pain of people suffering from heart disease, particularly angina pectores. Amyl nitrite widens the body's blood vessels and acts as a short term stimulant. The capsules containing amyl nitrite give off a popping or snapping noise when crushed so that the vapors can be inhaled — hence the pseudonyms, "poppers" or "snappers."

When used for non-medical purposes, amyl nitrite has gotten the reputation for being the "love drug" in recognition of its supposed ability to enhance pleasure when inhaled towards climax of the love making act. Amyl nitrite has been restricted to a "prescription only" drug which caused pleasure seekers to look for substitutes.

Notes, Comments & Ideas

...Your kids want to talk with you about alcohol and other drugs

INHALANTS — BUTYL NITRITE

Butyl nitrite is not currently classified as a drug but its effects mimic amyl nitrite. It goes by some weird sounding street names such as locker room, rush, joc, and aroma which evolved because of butyl nitrite's tendency to smell like an overused pair of dirty athletic socks.

Problems from short term use of these nitrites are fairly minor — headaches, feelings of pressure behind the eyes, nausea and faintness. According to users, these are outweighed by the instantaneous rush of dizziness and exhilaration.

When used frequently and over a long period of time, the nitrites can be downright dangerous. They increase pressure on the nerves and blood cells in the eyes and contribute to the chances of getting glaucoma, a serious eye disorder. Nitrites can also damage red blood cells, quite often causing anemia since the blood can not carry proper amounts of oxygen.

Notes, Comments & Ideas

STEROIDS

ANABOLIC STEROIDS

Notes, Comments & Ideas

Anabolic steroids — the muscle builders — were developed in the 1960's as a synthetic version of the male hormone, testosterone. As a legitimate prescription drug, its uses include treatment for certain types of cancer, rheumatoid arthritis, and for a disease called hereditary angiodema. Some brand names are Dianabol, Mestoranum, Anavar, Orabolin, Winstrol Vigorex, Virilon, Testred.

Anabolic steroids started to be used by athletes in the United States after it became known how these drugs helped Russian and East German athletes dominate some international track and field events.

Despite the fact that there are numerous bad side effects which appear quite quickly, many high school athletes have felt that the rewards were worth the risks and used steroids to build their muscles and strength. The urge to win or to get an athletic scholarship for college seemed more important than worrying about warnings of bad things that could happen sometime in the future.

A robust business exists in the manufacture and sale of illicit steroids. Europe, South America and Mexico are suspected points of origin. These supplies, when added to the output of a number of clandestine U.S. laboratories, results in total sales of over $50 million annually.

There is a substantial black market in steroids. Much of the product is illegally imported in pill form from Mexico. Remember, the ever present question

...Your kids want to talk with you about alcohol and other drugs

STEROIDS — ANABOLIC STEROIDS

when users pop an illegal pill into their mouths is "What's really in it?"

The use of steroids creates problems that show up quickly — acne, lessening sexual desires, rashes, and aggressive behavior. The problems from long term use are serious and can be life threatening:

- Cardiovascular — high blood pressure and hardening of the arteries.

- Liver and kidneys — preliminary research indicates the possibility of steroids being a factor in the development of liver and kidney cancers.

- Bone growth — steroids can slow or stop bone growth in young athletes, both skeletal and that of arms and legs, which combine to create a down sized adult.

- Sexual Dysfunction — lowered sperm counts and shriveled testicles can create impaired sexual functioning, often accompanied by a lack of interest in sexual activity. Also, some male users gain enlarged breasts and prostate glands. After prolonged use, women may expect development of a beard and mustache, plus a hairy chest and a tendency toward baldness. Their voices can become deeper and some evidence suggests that steroids increase the risk of breast cancer.

- Aggression — Although some athletes feel the aggressiveness caused by steroid use is an important factor in the business of winning, the change in the user's personality is often observed as abrasive and disagreeable. This is part of a pattern of extreme mood swings, which at the low end create anxiety, insomnia, and a tendency to make erratic decisions.

Notes, Comments & Ideas

STEROIDS —ANABOLIC STEROIDS

So far, the scientific community has not done much research on available steroids and this already long list of negative side effects may become longer as more is known.

To recognize signs of use, here are some things to look out for:

- Rapid gain in muscle size
- Acne
- Bloating in the face and swelling in the feet
- Focus on working out
- Changes in personality, ranging from aggressiveness to depression
- Inappropriate reaction to minor problems

Since anabolic steroid use is banned in all high school, college, and professional sports and because their use over time can be so dangerous, parents should, without question, add them to the list of "never to be used" drugs.

Notes, Comments & Ideas

DEAR PARENTS PLEASE...

Family Intervention

Sometimes the "no use" rule doesn't work; discouraging after so much work! But all is not lost.

Let's imagine a 15-year-old named Paul who comes home one evening reeking of beer. Or maybe bits of marijuana and rolling papers have been found in the pocket of his jacket. What should be done?

The answer is to intervene and take immediate action. If the family abstinence rule is broken, punishment should be as severe as that reserved for violation of any "most important family rule." If both parents are available, the matter can be most effectively handled as a joint effort, making clear again that for health reasons, absolutely no infraction of the drinking and drugging rule will be tolerated.

Let us hope by intervening and taking prompt action, Paul's parents will have convinced him to stay on track. And because they coupled the punishment with statements of love and anxiety for his well being, Paul felt his parents were being reasonable and accepted his punishment with good grace.

Over the years I have heard a fair number of recovered alcoholics say they drank alcoholically with their first drink. Let us say young Paul is one of these unfortunates. His craving for alcohol overrides family rules. He quickly becomes clever in concealing his drinking and often substitutes marijuana to avoid the smell of alcohol. His parents fail to see what is happening until some changes in Paul's behavior become quite obvious. His school grades have slipped, his appearance is sloppy and while he talks big, he accomplishes little. He seems surly and out of

Notes, Comments & Ideas

FAMILY INTERVENTION

sorts much of the time — so much so that his parents become convinced something is very wrong.

After they talk over the situation, they decide something must be done but feel unqualified to make a diagnosis or a decision on a course of action. So they seek professional help to evaluate what is going on with Paul. Are the changes in Paul just a part of adolescence? Or are they, as his parents fear, because he is using drugs?

Whatever the cause, they know they must intervene again. Paul admits nothing, but after much pressure agrees to see a professional. The chemical dependency counselor is not fooled and is able to get some facts out of Paul. Later, in a meeting with Paul and his parents, the results of the evaluation are discussed. It is decided to accept Paul's promise to quit using marijuana and alcohol with a further promise to go for treatment if he fails.

For a time, it appears Paul has conquered his need to drink or smoke. His grades improve along with his general attitude. Just as his parents' anxiety begins to subside, it becomes obvious that once again things are not right. His mother receives a call from the school counselor, who expresses the concern various teachers feel about Paul's attitude and behavior.

Another intervention is planned; this time it is to take place at school and is to be led by the chemical dependency counselor. Paul's parents, followed by the school counselor, give factual examples of his actions which break both the school's and the family's rules. His parents couple each of their examples with short expressions of how Paul's actions made them feel.

Notes, Comments & Ideas

...Your kids want to talk with you about alcohol and other drugs

Last, the chemical dependency professional reminds Paul of his promise to go for help if he failed to be able to keep his word.

Because the interveners are so well prepared and understand the process so well, they succeed in convincing Paul he is sick and needs to enter a local treatment center. There it is hoped that he will come to understand the positive possibilities of life without alcohol or drugs, and that he will go on to involve himself in Alcoholics Anonymous, which can help him lead a normal productive life. Nowadays among the several types of AA meetings are many for young people of Paul's age.

Not so many years ago, it was generally believed that nothing could be done for someone suffering from the disease of chemical dependency unless he or she hit some kind of "bottom" — a time when the world comes crashing down, sweeping away the denial of trouble. It was only then that the victim could be expected to seek help.

We now know that early intervention is effective and because Paul's parents knew how to enlist help, their intervention worked. We leave Paul with the hope that the treatment center will be successful in starting him on the road to recovery.

Chemical dependency, which includes alcoholism and/or addiction to other mood altering drugs, is a treatable disease. We have learned that it is progressive and can be fatal. Early intervention is a method of short circuiting the progression, sometimes saving years of misery for the addicted person and for those close to him or her.

Notes, Comments & Ideas

Dr. Vernon Johnson's book, *I'll Quit Tomorrow*, describes the early intervention process in detail. By developing the process, Dr. Johnson has saved countless lives. Families throughout the world have reason to be grateful to him. The Johnson Institute in Minneapolis may be able to recommend sources of professional help in your area if you are thinking about an intervention and do not know where to go for guidance.

Notes, Comments & Ideas

DEAR PARENTS PLEASE...

Final Thoughts on Connected Issues

SUPPORTING THE NON-USER

Notes, Comments & Ideas

Like almost everything written about the teenage drinking and drugging epidemic, this book has so far dealt only with ways to prevent or deal with problems caused by the user. No space has been allotted to the "non-user." These girls and boys are part of another "silent majority." They deserve and need support and attention. A child's decision *not to use* in our teenage society can be lonely. The pressures to use by peers can go on and on, often casting doubt and derision on the wisdom of the abstinence decision. To remain steadfast takes courage and strength of character. The users, on the other hand, and particularly those in trouble, get virtually all the attention. Having to deal with students who have broken school alcohol and drug rules is time consuming for the faculty and administration and disrupts the entire educational process.

Some years ago, FCD developed a program to recognize and support the non-user. We have held several conferences to explore the concept, including possibilities for non-using students to exert reverse peer pressure in order to persuade others that a life free of any mood altering chemicals has many rewards and is worth seeking. One of the students attending a conference was a junior at a large Southern day school. You can imagine our delight in learning that he had run for, and won, the office of student president on the platform of "I Choose Not To Use."

Alcohol and other drugs often may come up as a part of some family discussion or maybe as the main topic. A parent could well use these times to support and compliment a child who is living by the family abstinence rule, "I just want you to know how happy you are making us and how proud we are of you." A few moments spent in this way can pay large dividends in bolstering courage and determination to remain steadfast to the commitment of non-use.

TEACHING CHILDREN RESPONSIBLE DRINKING — A BAD IDEA

I do not agree with people who think it's a good idea to teach children to drink "responsibly" in the hope that this will prevent trouble later on. Beside the fact that I am uncertain what drinking responsibly means, it seems to me that parents should be able to find something a bit more constructive to teach their children. With a good percentage of kids, the effects of that "bottle of beer with dad," or that "glass of wine with supper," are remembered with sufficient pleasure to stir up thoughts of surrender to the pressure of school mates to join in their drinking and pot smoking parties.

The physical makeup of some people causes a craving for alcohol which starts with their very first drink. At a recent party, one of my dinner partners was a woman who I had not met before. In getting acquainted, she asked what I did for work. As so often happens, when I told her, she made me privy to the problems alcohol caused for her family. As far as she knew, her father had been a teetotaler all of his life until her mother had died at an early age. After the funeral, her father disappeared and was found dead drunk three days later. She went on to say that

Notes, Comments & Ideas

thereafter he never gained control of his drinking and was killed by alcohol a few years later.

Drinking alcoholically from the first drink on occurs more frequently with the young. **Children are less well equipped physically, spiritually and emotionally to fight off alcohol's grip as it seeks to destroy the adolescent years.** Wouldn't you agree that it makes more sense to teach abstinence than to run the risk of disaster by teaching a child to "drink responsibly?"

MODERATE DRINKING — A GROWN-UPS RIGHT

Adults, particularly parents, are supposed to set examples for children when it comes to drinking alcohol. Some say parents send the wrong message to their kids if they drink at all. I don't agree. Why should parents and other grown-ups refrain from an adult activity which is legal and can be pleasurable? Drinking in moderation has been a useful social lubricant and easer of tensions and fatigue for centuries.

Children should understand they can also enjoy moderate drinking when they reach the legal drinking age and drinking is no longer a threat to their growing-up process. It seems to me the young these days are allowed to do many grown-up things before they are ready. Parents might do well to try treating kids more like kids and raise them with sensible family rules.

FINAL THOUGHTS ON CONNECTED ISSUES

A WISER "WAR ON DRUGS"

Notes, Comments & Ideas

Hardly anyone has much good to say about the government's costly effort to cut off the flow of drugs into our country. Many feel that more emphasis on cutting demand through education and treatment would be a more fruitful way to spend our tax dollars. There is widespread support for increasing the number of police available to patrol areas of high crime and violence. One must hope the addition of 100,000 police officers called for in the 1994 Crime Bill will become a reality.

Some well known men and women have argued, sometimes passionately, for the legalization of many unlawful drugs. Currently, two legal drugs — alcohol and nicotine — are directly or indirectly responsible for nearly 400,000 deaths each year. It seems ridiculous to even consider adding to a huge death toll by encouraging increased use of other health damaging and often potentially fatal drugs. Legalization would send a powerful message to the young — several million of whom are already harmfully dependent on easy-to-get, but illegal (for them), nicotine and alcohol. We simply don't need to make drugs like cocaine and marijuana cheaper and easier to get, or to imply in any way that their use is not a potential health hazard.

Instead, we believe that the major portion of the annual multi-billion dollar "War on Drugs" budget should be allocated for an all media public education blitz, designed and targeted primarily at parents. With knowledge, parents gain the power to talk sensibly to children about the truly dangerous health consequences of using

...Your kids want to talk with you about alcohol and other drugs

113

alcohol, nicotine and other mood altering drugs. By adding a good dose of parental love, it's quite possible that a family no-use by minors rule will then be successful.

Helping to curb a huge national health problem is the responsibility of every family. Considering all that is said about the breakdown of the American family these days, there's every reason for grandparents, aunts and uncles to do their bit and become a part of a kinder, gentler and wiser "War on Drugs."

POSTSCRIPT

By now I hope that you are thinking of alcoholism and/or other drug addiction as a disease with the potential to harm equal to that of the most dreaded illnesses such as polio, meningitis, hepatitis B, cancer or heart disease. I hope also you'll agree that a family "no use" rule can generally be made to work if parents know the facts and use them with that special kind of love that only they have for their children.

I have been blessed by a wonderful group of grandchildren and step-grandchildren. I enjoy all of them and love each one dearly. One is a five year old boy. He is a wonderful looking young man, outgoing and energetic. He is at the exciting age when changes in what he can say and do seem to happen almost daily. I know he can be an exasperating handful for his parents, but my limited grandfatherly time with him is pure joy. He shines with wellness which makes me think of the pitfalls that face him in the years before he is grown. It is comforting to know that his parents are determined to teach him to make the right

Notes, Comments & Ideas

decisions to protect his health. I know that lurking inside him and my other grandchildren may be inherited genes which makes alcohol use something to be worried about. I know all my family understands these dangers. I wonder sometimes if things would have turned out differently had I grown up when more was known about the addictions and had my parents been able to give me the facts. I certainly would like to think so. No one chooses to become addicted. The journey through alcoholism is a desperate time which is horribly painful for both the sick individual and for those closest to him or her. I am enormously grateful to be a survivor. And though I live one day at a time, I hope that by God's grace to have other chances to beat the drum for parent action on a health problem that is clearly theirs to solve.

Notes, Comments & Ideas

DEAR PARENTS PLEASE...

Suggested Reading

I'LL QUIT TOMORROW
—Vernon E. Johnson, $14.95

Harpers & Row Publishers, Inc.
10 East 53rd St.
New York, NY 10022

Stages of dependency and addiction—early intervention. Explains psychological and emotional problems.

UNDER THE INFLUENCE
—Dr. James R. Milam
& Katherine Ketcham, $12.95

Madrona Publishers, Inc.
P.O. Box 22667
Seattle, Washington 98122

Physiology, not psychology, determines whether one drinker will become addicted to alcohol and another will not.

FACTS ABOUT DRUG ABUSE
—Barry Stimmel, M.D.

The Haworth Medical Press
10 Alice Street
Binghampton, NY 13904-1580

Easy-to-understand, non-technical language. All you need to know to make rational decisions on alcohol and other drug use.

Additional Reading

SUGGESTED READING

Additional Reading

_____
_____
_____
_____
_____
_____
_____
_____
_____
_____
_____
_____
_____
_____
_____
_____
_____
_____
_____
_____
_____

...Your kids want to talk with you about alcohol and other drugs

DEAR PARENTS PLEASE...

Additional Resources

TOUGH LOVE OFFICE
1069 Doylestown, PA 18901
(215) 348-7090

ALCOHOLICS ANONYMOUS / ALANON / ALATEEN
Local Phone Book

NATIONAL DRUG ABUSE CENTER
(Training Materials)
5330 Wisconsin Ave.
N.W., Suite 1600
Washington, DC 20015

HAZELDEN EDUCATIONAL MATERIAL
Pleasant Valley Road
Box 176
Center City, MN 55012-0176
(800) 328-9000

AMERICAN COUNCIL FOR DRUG EDUCATION
5820 Hubbard Drive
Rockville, MD 20857
(301) 984-5700
or
135 East 64th Street
New York, NY 10021
(212) 758-8060

PACIFIC INSTITUTE FOR RESEARCH AND EVALUATION
7101 Wisconsin Ave
Suite 612
Bethesda, MD 20814
(310) 986-0303 or (800) 258-2766

THE JOHNSON INSTITUTE
7205 Ohms Lane
Minneapolis, MN 55439
1-800-231-5165

Additional Resources

...Your kids want to talk with you about alcohol and other drugs